Please visit our web site at: www.garethstevens.com
For a free color catalog describing Gareth Stevens Publishing's list of high-quality books
and multimedia programs, call 1-800-542-2595 (USA) or 1-800-387-3178 (Canada).
Gareth Stevens Publishing's fax: (414) 332-3567.

Library of Congress Cataloging-in-Publication Data

Laschütza, Susanne.
   [Klaus Fledermaus. English]
   Nat the bat / text and illustrations by Susanne Laschütza.
     p. cm.
   Summary: Nat, a bat with unusual tastes, ventures out from his church tower home
all by himself and has an encounter with Paul the dog.
   ISBN 0-8368-3573-5 (lib. bdg.)
   [1. Bats—Fiction. 2. Dogs—Fiction.] I. Title.
PZ7.L3268Nat   2003
[E]—dc21   2002036496

This North American edition first published in 2003 by
Gareth Stevens Publishing
A World Almanac Education Group Company
330 West Olive Street, Suite 100
Milwaukee, WI 53212 USA

Gareth Stevens editor: JoAnn Early Macken
Gareth Stevens art direction: Tammy Gruenewald

This edition © 2003 by Gareth Stevens, Inc. First published as *Klaus Fledermaus* by Dachs-Verlag, Austria.
Original edition © 2001 by Dachs-Verlag GmbH, Biberhaufenweg 100/38, A-1220 Vienna, Austria.

Printed in the United States of America

1 2 3 4 5 6 7 8 9 07 06 05 04 03

NAT the BAT

by Susanne Laschütza

Gareth Stevens Publishing
A WORLD ALMANAC EDUCATION GROUP COMPANY

High in the top of the town church tower, Nat the Bat looked out at the world for the first time. Mama held him in her wings and squeaked with joy. "Good little bat!" she said.

As he grew, Nat played with the other baby bats. They stretched and tumbled among the rafters, training their wings to fly.

Before long, the young bats fluttered through the church tower. The time had come for their mothers to take them out on their first night flight.

"Stick together," Mama called out. "No fooling around or flying off."

As they flew, Nat noticed a tiny house near two big buildings. "What is that little house for?" he asked.

"That is a doghouse," Mama answered. "A mean dog named Paul lives there."

"Where is he now?" asked Nat.

"He roams around the countryside at night," Mama said. "Watch out for him!"

At the edge of the forest, the young bats began their first insect hunt.
They learned to use sound to find prey while they flew. Nat chased
after a moth. Snap! He caught it and started to chew.

Mama flew by. "How do you like it, Nat?" she asked.

Nat choked down the moth. "Yuck! It's disgusting!" he replied. "I'll
never eat anything so awful again."

"Nonsense!" Mama said. "All good little bats eat insects."

Back in the church tower, the young bats bragged about their first hunt. Only Nat kept quiet.

An old bat winked at him and asked, "Didn't you have any luck?"

"I caught a moth," Nat said. "But I didn't like the taste."

"Give it time," the old bat said. "Or maybe you'd like the taste of blood, like the bats in South America."

Nat wrinkled his nose. "Blood?" he asked.

"Yes, like vampire bats. They drink blood instead of eating insects," the old bat said.

That morning when the Sun rose, all the bats went to sleep — all except Nat, that is. He swung from side to side, bumping into bats as he dangled. Bang! He bumped into Mama. Boom! He bumped into the bat on the other side.

"Excuse me," he said. "I'm sorry!"

But Mama and the other bat bumped into the bats next to them. Soon all the bats were wide awake.

Bats muttered. Bats grumbled. Bats rubbed their eyes.

"Nat, what's the matter?" Mama asked.

"I can't sleep," Nat said.

"That's ridiculous!" Mama said. "All good little bats sleep in the daytime."

That evening when the Sun went down, all the bats woke up — all except Nat, that is. Mama and the other bats got ready for their next insect hunt.

"Nat," they called. "Wake up! It's time to eat!"

But Nat slept on. He would not wake up.

Mama smiled at Nat. "Let him sleep," she said. "All good little bats need their rest."

When Nat woke up, all the other bats were gone. He thought about going to look for them, but they were probably out hunting insects. He shuddered. He wrinkled his nose. "Maybe that old bat was right," Nat said to himself. "Maybe I am a vampire bat." Nat decided to find out.

Nat flew over fields and meadows, searching for a hearty vampire meal. Below him, a flock of sheep grazed in the moonlight. Nat looked for the fattest, juiciest one. Then he dove toward the sheep, screeching all the way.

Just as Nat was about to bite, the sheep moved. Nat crashed to the ground and lay there, stunned.

The sound of panting woke him up. He opened his eyes. A big dog stood before him with his mouth wide open and his tongue hanging out. It was Paul!

Nat struggled to get up. His whole body shook with fear. He opened his mouth to scream and felt blood dripping out. He must have bitten his tongue when he fell.

Finally, Nat cried out. The dog backed up. The hairs on his neck stood up.

The dog whined. He turned around and ran away. Something must have frightened him. Nat couldn't believe his luck.

Nat hated the taste of blood. All he wanted was to get back to the church tower. Mama would be getting worried.

"I'm so glad you're home," Mama said. "Are you all right?"

"I'm fine," Nat said. "But I'm very hungry."

"Hungry enough to eat a moth?" Mama asked.

"Two moths, a fly, and some nice, fresh mosquitoes," Nat said.

Mama held him in her wings and squeaked with joy. "Good little bat!" she said.